Camille Comes Unglued

Dr. Jennifer Lagier

Also by Jennifer Lagier

Dystopia Playlist, Cyberwit, 2020.

Trumped Up Election, Xi Draconis Books, 2019.

Camille Mobilizes, FutureCycle Press, 2018.

Like a B Movie, FutureCycle Press, 2018.

Harbingers, Blue Light Press, 2016.

Scene of the Crime, Evening Street Press, 2016.

Camille Abroad, FutureCycle Press, 2016.

Where We Grew Up, FutureCycle Press, 2015.

Camille Vérité, FutureCycle Press, 2014.

Acknowledgments

Cover art by Gene McCormick.

The author is grateful to the following publications for originally publishing some of these poems:

"Tiny Agonies," *I Am Not a Silent Poet*

"Everywhere," *In Between Hangovers*

"Meltdown," *Winedrunk Sidewalk*

"Crazy," *Winedrunk Sidewalk*

"Goddess-zilla Gets Woke," *Winedrunk Sidewalk*

"Dead-before-death Gang," *Winedrunk Sidewalk*

"New Complexities," *I Am Not a Silent Poet*

"No Resistance, No Thoughts of Their Own," *Winedrunk Sidewalk*

"The truth will set you free, but first it will piss you off."

—Gloria Steinem

Contents

Tiny Agonies

Camille sips hot coffee,
scrolls through Internet headlines:
Porn Star Says Trump Bad in Bed;
Nuclear War, Extreme Weather
Top List of 2018 Threats;
Marathon Running Mom, 10-Year-Old
Boy Latest Flu Victims;
China space station packed with
'CANCEROUS chemicals'
to crash into Earth 'within MONTHS'.

She is fed up starting every morning
with elevated blood pressure, wanting
to vaporize Washington DC,
exterminate White House residents,
migrate to a remote forest
or desert island
to escape rampant stupidity.
There aren't enough bong hits
to erase oppressive, offensive reality.

Instead, she drags out magic marker,
a huge sheet of poster board,
creates a protest sign
with scathing message, pointed graphics.
She'll share her anger and energy
with vibrant, vocal, voting females.
at the local Women's March,
Together, they will oust inept,

sexist clowns currently in power,
bring back intelligent, humane behavior,
take over all levels of government,
make the world sane.

#Time's Up

"One collapses and surrenders..." – Charles Bukowski

Camille looks forward to the R. Kellys
and Harvey Weinsteins,
predators who can't keep it in their pants,
being apprehended, convicted, jailed,
encountering their own rapists.

Count her among millions of women
no longer willing to shut the fuck up
about molestation, degradation,
denied career advancement
for another's sick pleasure.

Watch her harness
every iota of energy
to help bring down sexist abusers,
facilitate the dismantling
of patriarchal, enabling culture.

#Time's Up, assholes, she thinks.
Welcome to a brave new world
where women make and enforce rules
to ensure a level playing field,
gender-blind social justice.

The Beast

Low blood sugar, jetlag
caffeine overdose,
rebellious hormones
bring out Camille's worst.

She transforms from assertive Amazon
into shrill harpy, craves confrontation,
aches to draw blood, rip away pound
of a politician's quivering flesh.

Friends recognize the danger signs:
fanged rejoinders, frenzied pacing.
For self-preservation, they've learned
to give her acres of space.

Election night aftermath
only aggravates volatile temperament,
unleashes monster behavior as she morphs
into vindictive, fury-pumped beast.

Everywhere

"I can't get no satisfaction..." – Rolling Stones

Camille starts her day at Starbucks
where the body-pierced, tattooed barista
is unable to correctly fill her simple order
for a latte, flubs counting change.

Later, she navigates crowded freeway.
Drivers wildly change lanes without
using their signals; slow cars obstruct traffic.
Cal-trans blocks the exit she needs.

Swerving to avoid a moron,
she watches as $5.00 of designer coffee
splashes into her lap, onto the seat where
it stains beige sweater, gray upholstery.

At her support group meeting,
she recites the opening preamble,
seethes, shares an inventory of grievances,
is anything but serene.

Meltdown

*"What is there to say about former Mayor of New York City
Rudy Giuliani that hasn't been farted into a bag and fed to a
demon for punishment?" – Daily Kos*

Camille reads Rudy's latest mental meanderings
in response to pussy-grabber-in-chief's
senile behavior, tone-deaf remarks.
The phrase "Takes one to know one"
sticks in her mind.

Co-conspiring, seditious white men
discover privilege is not permanent.
As Mueller's investigation uncovers
layers of perjured malfeasance,
indictments gnaw at their heels.

Giuliani's dementia escalates,
manifests itself in social media postings
as he incriminates his oblivious client and self.
The shit show unravels before Camille's eyes,
pervasive treason revealed.

Her Golden Years

Now that Camille is pushing 70,
solicitation phone calls are never-ending.
Her mailbox overflows with ads
for cremation, hearing aids,
assisted living.

Doctors refuse to listen
to descriptions of symptoms.
They attribute aches and pains
to advancing age.
Rarely bother to order
diagnostic blood tests or x-rays.

Increasingly fragile, she
no longer jogs or pumps iron,
swallows handfuls of supplements,
can dislocate or break bones
with the simple act
of just bending over.

Crazy

Camille notices a woman in the pharmacy
check-out line as she unloads her basket:
home pregnancy test, bag of Doritos,
midnight blue eyeliner,
toy Jedi light saber.

She flaunts chipped ebony toenails,
wears faded Levi's.
Her torn Metallica tee shirt
clings by a thread,
has seen better days.

A drunk, homeless man hits Camille up
for a dollar as she walks to her car.
She contemplates the unraveling social asylum,
everyone looking for whatever erases or numbs,
doing what they can to get by.

Not Worth It

Camille hasn't the patience
for more complications,
decides to swear off earnest
organizers, abrasive civic
meetings, ethical problems,
high maintenance men.

In this culture of cruelty,
she chooses not to participate
in the ongoing Stanford experiment of corruption and power,
concentrates on creation,
entertains spoiled dogs, surrounds herself
with Big Sur beauty, blooming Columbine, nourishing friends.

Goddess-zilla Gets Woke

"You look prettier when you smile!"
strangers shout at Camille as they pass.
At professional meetings,
her supervisor reprimands
when she objects to interruptions,
says she sounds shrill.

A creepy ex-boyfriend
Emails out of the blue,
asks for her telephone number
so he can reconnect, share details
about his adventuresome life.
She deletes his message,
makes sure he is blocked.

Rage bubbles inside her
from a lifetime of indoctrination,
demands she remain invisible, acquiescent.
Fury fuels her awakening,
a decision to break glass ceilings,
overthrow repressive conditioning,
achieve radical change.

Grabbing her pussy hat
and picket sign,
she joins her sisters
as they march,
link arms and chant,
confront their oppressors,
take back the streets.

Something That Will Help

"...just a shot away..." – Rolling Stones

Camille discovers cannabis tincture
at the local dispensary,
credits this magic potion
for altering perspective,
lifting her spirits.

THC erases current events,
eases anxiety,
mollifies anger,
transforms froggy lovers
into erotic Prince Charmings.

At night, a dropper or two
insures unbroken sleep,
provocative dreams,
chemical Valhalla
to survive until morning.

The Dead-Before-Death Gang

They wear geezerdom
like scruffy badges of honor,
snarl at women who enter their lair,
a fetid saloon for cranky,
resentful men who have succumbed
to stale testosterone poisoning.

Looking in, Camille sees a gang
of the living dead.
They drive away all who care,
with their pissing and moaning,
communally nurse escalating
bitterness, grudges.

They fester and stew,
obsess over ancient, exaggerated wrongs,
take privilege for granted,
imagine vindictive revenge.
The 21st Century
passes them by.

Men Write the Same Letter

Men who wander off the reservation
find their way under Camille's skin,
repeat predictable phrases:
Let's keep things light.
Don't ever call my home.
I'll never file for divorce.

She thinks of them as
randy neighborhood tom cats,
slinking to her door
for a quickie hand-out
when it fits their need,
nowhere to be found
when she's in the mood.

Despite spam filter,
their random communications
reappear as rogue emails
to be blocked, deleted, ignored.

Who knows what triggers
whims for nostalgic reunion?
She's learned to build higher fences,
change the locks and combinations,
take care of herself.

Turned and Walked Away

*"I truly loved you, put no one above you. Now I'm walking
away." – Jonny Lang*

Camille's fire has burnt itself out.
Lovers who once left her aching
now fail to satisfy, just piss her off.

In her thirties, she moistened
as she imagined sexual conquests,
erotic, fantasy fucks.

Now her hip joints ache.
Exhaustion overwhelms by 9 p.m.
Age makes her its unwilling bitch.

Romance seems too much work.
All she wants is peace and quiet,
a quaint little cottage with stabilized rent.

Edges

Camille has honed her body
to hard bone and muscle,
is ready for the fight of her life,
casts off zaftig softness.

No more optimistic denials
to insulate against rising fascism, violence.
She transforms into tough Amazon,
her lean physique, a taut, knuckled fist.

Age and impatience erode politeness,
acquiescence of the unacceptable.
She aches to rumble, take down
every dangerous political despot.

You Grow Transformed

Camille hasn't felt cold
since she turned 55.
When sexy men approach,
latent estrogen flares,
lights her up like a torch.
She flushes from head to toe,
squirms and grows damp.

In bed, however,
intimate body parts no longer
fit together smoothly,
bring sensual pleasure
as in the past.

There's little on the market
to erase hard years,
rejuvenate what invisibly pinches,
spasms and sags.

Camille's fickle flesh
is uncooperative,
thwarts desire,
has closed up shop,
gone out on strike.

No Resistance, No Thoughts of Their Own

Camille knows it's pure masochism
watching talking bobble heads
on Sunday morning news shows,
hearing debates on whether
Individual No. 1 is racist
or just deflecting public attention
from impending impeachment.

Moscow Mitch and his lock-step clique
of corrupt GOP clones
can be counted on to parrot
the party line as dictated
by Sean Hannity and Faux News,
red meat to his ravening pack,
whatever distraction is necessary
to redirect outrage onto a new target.

This is how democracy falls.

Reality Check

"A wise woman likes but doesn't love, listens but doesn't believe and leaves before she is left." – Marilyn Monroe

Camille passes shop sign:
The Soiled Dove Bath House,
shakes her head at the sexist label,
ponders how society persists
in getting it wrong.

Puritanical hypocrites ignore
her healthy libido,
diverse love life,
sensual proclivities,
limber potential.

Her fire might dim
but will never die,
still radiates heat when
encountering sexy men
despite gray hair and wrinkles.

Camille Comes Unglued

"It's a complex issue because one has to think, well there's a host body and that host body has to have a certain amount of rights because at the end of the day it is that body that that carries this entire other body to term. But there is an additional life there."— Florida state Rep. Jose Oliva

Camille reads the quote, becomes incandescent.
Despises arrogant misogyny, ignorant belief that
she's nothing more than a baby container.
Vows to support progressive women candidates
so every female can control her own body.

She wonders how men would react
if re-designated as insentient hosts,
each drop of semen conferred with
person-hood rights that outweighed
male intentions and interests.

If it impacted them, would obtuse dudes
oppose governmental interference,
unqualified legislators in the driver's seat
making decisions regarding
another's reproductive organs?

Camille listens to a procession
of smug, self-righteous old guys
pontificate on the sanctity of the pre-born,
discovers she is fresh out of fucks to give,
grows increasingly livid with rage.

Sleep Alone

Camille has replaced lovers
with two snuggly dogs,
an extra-large pillow.
Finds she prefers
sprawling comfortably alone
in her own king-size bed.

At night, she can stretch,
snore if she wishes.
Let erotic dreams bloom.
Slip one foot out
from under the quilt
without male obstruction.

Drained

It's one of those mornings
when Camille needs to isolate,
meditate and restore.
No more hysterical headlines,
hate-infused social media diatribes,
depressing global warming predictions.

While she banishes doom and gloom,
her sated lover sleeps late.
Surrounded by lazy dogs,
he snuggles deeper
among rumpled blankets,
snores from the bedroom.

Camille savors Greek yogurt and berries,
deletes emails from political candidates
begging for money,
pours a cup of mocca java coffee,
smiles at passing hummingbirds,
hides in her flowering garden.

Genesis Extravaganza

Camille squeezes into her orchestra seat
at San Francisco's Regency Ballroom.
It's exactly the sausage fest she expected:
at least six bald, slogan tee shirted men
for every outnumbered woman.
Around her, beer-guzzling early Genesis buffs,
a sea of enlarged prostates, involuntary celibates,
potential erectile dysfunction.
She comforts herself with the thought
there won't be uncomfortable lines
at too few women's restrooms.

On stage, five French Canadian musicians
with long, swinging hair
wearing white yoga pants perform
framed by a slide show of obscure artwork.
She can't recognize a single song
but enjoys the look of mesmerized joy
on her partner's ecstatic face.
Bizarre costumes, interminable drum riffs,
flailing arms, clouds of cannabis vapors
envelope sardine-packed audience.
A balcony filled with LSD tripping
retreads from the seventies sing along
with the band, dance their hearts out.

New Complexities

Camille's pleasure portal
has gone on strike,
locked the door,
thrown away the key,
refuses to admit
digits, appendages,
even a sex toy.

When she experiments
with new positions,
her insides shriek, shred and bleed.
Pricey hormone creams,
marijuana lubricants,
anti-inflammatory ointments
fail to restore what's broken inside.

What the fuck? Camille wonders
after one more painful failure,
retires erotic gymnastics
that no longer bring satisfaction,
promotes foreplay to the main event,
ruefully reminds herself
there is always an upside.

Love Beds

Camille inventories scenes of erotic adventures:
the canal bank where a high school sweetheart
taught how to bring a man pleasure,
once on a stranger's pool table,
sprawled across the deck of an anchored yacht,
upon a sun-warmed rock in high sierras
overlooking green and gold Alpine meadow.

She has made love in swimming pools,
jacuzzi baths, hot tubs, the back seat
of her first husband's Mustang,
on a blanket in the middle
of her father's orchard
between rows of flowering almonds.

Lovemaking these days
requires more preparation:
steroid ointment, estrogen cream,
clean sheets, a comfortable bed,
orthopedic pillows, CBD tincture
to alleviate arthritic hips.

Camille Hits the Wall

It's week ten of sheltering in place.
Camille's stylish hairdo has devolved
to a silver tangle of cowlicks, split ends.
Her scarlet fingers and toes revert
to hangnails, ragged cuticles.
Thick calluses reclaim the soles of her feet.
The novelty of free time has worn off.
She is sick of reruns, has cleaned and organized
every cupboard and closet, dead-headed flowers,
scoured the garden of weeds.

Once obsessed over stylish couture, dangly earrings,
now she worries about having an adequate supply
of toilet paper, nitrile gloves, an assortment of masks.
Grocery shopping is conducted online with Doordash delivery,
or after suiting up in protective gear as if walking in space.
Security guards monitor the store entrance.
One-way aisles are labeled with arrows and signs,
warn shoppers to remain at least six feet apart.
Checkout lines lengthen as clerks behind plexiglass shields
sanitize counters, credit card keypad between customers.
Back home, she wipes down each purchase,
strips to shower, washes what she's worn.

Each day, when walls close in upon her,
confinement chafes, irritability blossoms.
She reminds herself how lucky she is
to still have income, health, a helpful partner,
large yard, spacious home with tons of books,
a writing room for herself.

Your Friends

Camille's cronies call each other goddesses,
dress in exotic gowns,
wear sparkling tiaras,
are the subjects of envious gossip,
hang out at bohemian bars
in the wilds of Big Sur.

They have each other's back,
listen without judgement,
commiserate during breakups,
hookups, illness, infirmity,
financial hardship,
family deaths.

They exchange house keys,
security codes,
Internet passwords
Share names of therapists,
publishing contacts,
massage technicians.

Vow to start
their own geriatric commune.
Can't imagine life
without this sisterhood
of sympathetic soulmates,
irreverent friends.

www.ingramcontent.com/pod-product-compliance
Lightning Source LLC
LaVergne TN
LVHW041130180726
843490LV00003B/1275